MONKS' FRUIT

MONKS' FRUIT

A.J. LEVIN

A Junction Book

NIGHTWOOD EDITIONS

ROBERTS CREEK, BC

2004

Nightwood Editions
R.R. #22, 3692 Beach Ave.
Roberts Creek, BC
Canada V0N 2W2

We gratefully acknowledge the support of the Canada Council for the Arts and the British Columbia Arts Council for our publishing program.

NATIONAL LIBRARY OF CANADA CATALOGUING IN PUBLICATION

Levin, A. J.
    Monks' fruit / A.J. Levin.

Poems.
"A Junction book".
ISBN 0-88971-202-6

        I. Title.

PS8573.E9644M66 2004   C811'.6   C2004-900798-X

to Karen

CONTENTS

Old-Age Benefits

The Show to End All

Baby Beef

Monks' Fruit

OLD-AGE BENEFITS

LETHE

After his futile CPR
I thought nothing enough.
Even hard to eat *shivah* veal
some neighbour kindly prepared.

Instead: in my hands
I find your gifts, a rain,
it reminds me there was
some use, loving my brother.

And reading in
your young paper eyes
(never twice the same
colour) a cherry-tea memory

of a past boy,
I want even more
to embrace you. Not to stop
you running but the Lethe.

ARCHAEOLOGY

Rare call from you, the pay phone
outside my door. Tonight's a festival,
Ramadan over. They're roasting
pungent camel meat over oil drums.
No Disney version of this.
Halal plates of spice flesh cleaned,
Father pontificates to the news,
argues with the papers—
WAR AT THE EAST OF THE EMPIRE—
twirling words as only mustachioed Muslims can.
Mother irons the striped briefs,
Uncle lurches through steam to adjacent rooms.
Here? Indifferent but you
wouldn't be cold in this February mist,
your sister the anaesthetist,
the search for numbness runs in the family.
I try to explain how snow can burn:
you don't quite believe it,
sitting at the edge of your family on. . .
funny, here we call it an ottoman,
maybe a Winnipeg couch.
Still poised for a cigarette and giving them up,
you're tempted back by blazing peace, as always.
Please escape sometimes too
in the cool of the black stout you first had here,
listen to the forbidden music,
vagabond through Cappadocia, Anatolia, or France.
Like that other Asian, Abraham,
safe but estranged in the furnace of his own land,
your country roots into you deeper than
a house perched at the rift-edge of a continent.

Another time, I call, another quake.
The radio says only years
before Istanbul is rubble.
Hey, Anaheim ain't Atlantis yet.
Oh?. . . it's in California.
Always the archaeologist, you tell me
on unclouded mornings you can see
a Dodecanese island from your dig.
They think maybe that was Atlantis.
Still no glimpse of the future? Anyway,
good to hear your shoulders don't buckle
under gravity of the historic death you uncover daily,
time-caked, Byzantine clay lamps,
and after tea, your fingers probe
today's gravel, yesterday's lunch,
come out scathed. Earth too can scald:
but the burns don't last as long.

DA VINCI

They say he can fly.
I say they will believe anything
the bishops speak out against.
I know these artists, especially
Firenze mountain-men. All his
inventions are a good reason for
labour-boys hewing and carting
and bending and panting, now
take the pantaloons off, soiled
by the dried cemetery mud.

They say he can see
the human soul, I say it's
blasphemy. He knows naked
bodies, their drawings in the
study where Hector works.
I'll not send him there next
time. I was saving the testoni
for hens, but God will bring.

They say he is a madman
but I am just a woman and can
not read. At least he has not
trifled with my time, reading
poems, like our foolish landlord.

They say he is a great man.
Why work markings onto paper,
tree corpse, when it could warm
the winter dust, our iced stew?

HENRY MOORE

Still after sharing a one-sheeted tight bed months
you doubted my motives for wanting photos of us,
even full-clothed colour tourist shots in museums—
while seventeen Henry Moores laughed on, polished
a cool naked black.
                       Later, in England, foreigners
will call the local girls *repressed*. But now, a month
after the art gallery, I am more uneasy than you
in the Yonge Street store. My first window into
the Catholic libido: red and black and leather
implements of penitence for cardinal sins.

POSEIDON

All-male Grade 10. We cut worms
open, prodded mirrored left and
right entrails. Behold: mostly guts
running straight down. How little
this taught me about the future,
slicing pickled, hermaphroditic bait
only helped foresee the evensidedness
of Wednesdays.

Moved up the food chain to perch.
Real soothsaying, ichthyomancy—
mine was pregnant. Unmattering
roe oozed through the cavity I
scalpelled since my lab-mate
was more scared of the future than me.
Everyone stood around my fish
and oohed, my teacher proud
as I was the father,
a happy Poseidon
after an orgy.

Later, elsewhere, a pub called The Perch, and you,
some Eastern river in your smile
only with more Celtic eyebrows, so:
I imagined us original, decadent
together, naked under purdah.

Only with new women have I done the dissection.
We lasted an exact life of two pregnancies, the same
eighteen months you always take and give.

TANTALUS IN THE CARIBOO

Lillooet is an innocent word—
on paper.

Yet my pay is
not paper but liver,
buckwheat grains
floated on stale water.

No getting around it. Everything is gold
and everything, everything has deserted me.
Say why the fool's gold prospers, washed
through this blasted prospector-Styx,
where yesterday only Shuswap traders
wandered, no white man to haggle with?
Today Haida harlots and Scotsmen, Yanks,
beard-headed Russians; they are the fools
who say in their hearts *There is gold!*
or *There!* Take this river cast under
judgement of these glowering fir-tree
tribes great and numerous. Mighty-
flowing fucking Fraser:
cool steals your pan,
pan thieves the gold, and
in the clear light of sun
washed so rare in this high valley,
the sheen becomes only
the glint of shed salmon scales,
not enough to eat or scrape
together even the gold dollar
I spent on drink the week
disembarked in foreign

Philadelphia, Greek
concept of brotherly love
meaning nothing in civil war.
Here, old moose jerky is
all you can give brother or foe,
make no mistake, they are the same man,
you will give it to him.
Or they will steal
your Nanaimo bars.
There are pointed guns.
If you are lucky they point
to a rabbit. Do not think
of the Spaniard who found
so much, no place to hide it
in a land where all you do
is swallowed, still hungry.
Once I saw a bat devour
a hummingbird. Who's
to say what is accident
in the unsettled land?

Yesterday I hallucinated
golden camels in the distance.

Sometimes, too, the gold
flies. I see it in the river
and it is only a glister
of eagles wary of us,
know we steal their meat,
the bronzeness of rabbit,
and the silver foxes.

So be it. My skin with time
has become metal, this country
is a Midas, minus a kingdom,
the river of gold we call sun
filters through the clouds
of pious alchemists in heaven,
turns you into the same steel
the Indians are born of. Like
drifts to like, the mineral
will find my pan. I
forged it out of pyrite.

Near my hut spotted owls
have made their chapel,
the primitive prayers not
from their talons, but what's
caught between them. Their food
is mine: sometimes I have sought
to eat their pellets. One catches
sometimes a mad glint off their eyes.
Or maybe my own desperate
reflection. But walls of bush
here are a tricky vanity
with a tricky mirror up top.
Wisdom comes from seeing
gold in heaven, the travelling preachers say,
but they still want their coin. And
I have followed the trail of rain
to this end of the world:
it never lands on
earthly waters.

What was the last town—Spuzzum?
Salmonwhet?—where the others
take joys?

And between the trees always
rum; or the spirit of the Indian,
the gold-plated mountain lion
claiming his share, whatever
the white gilt bear, who the
Indian claims is spirit, hasn't
staked. There are some things
for which even shotgun
and lead are not much use.

Sometimes I deliver drink.
It does the same to me.
On windless days, when
the green stocking atop a stave
in my front garden (dug up
by mountain beavers, once)
cowers listless; only then
do I think to the other sock,
left in ballroom haste with the
foreign girl, after my last strike
at the 29 Mile House Tavern.

ISAAC IN THE NORTH

Snow, ice, are melting at the head of March,
a mountain ram. The dead of night has been
adrift on the ice for so long. Now with melt
its corpse is ripe for stinking. Dead, too, in
a historical way, the frozen buds of star, iced
onto the dark tree four million years past. The
owl, bless his hungry soul, searches for life.

MACBETH IN BRAZIL

In a place filled with the poem
of human architecture, easy
not to be ambitious. Vines
flower eggplant-purple,
porcine vetch thrives
winter as autumn, a
drizzled heat falls

on a gutter dog
dark in the street
for whom there's
sleep no more.

MOSES

Moses down from Sinai
cast down the sewer of time
lives off his old-age benefits,
walks with two wood canes;

or maybe rides the number 7 bus,
Lear-flowers bobbing in his hat,
a strong wooden box wrapped with twine,
a dark blue toque against the rain.

PLATO'S BLUES

So I'm stuck here in Cecropia
with a lousy obol and a spinach tart
but I'm going down to Athens
in the back of Antisthenes' cart.

And I'll be famous there,
just like Homer and the Beatles,
singing *What's the Zeusing difference
between love and anything else?*

LAZARUS

John 11

Lazarus, wiping the four days' dirt, blowflies
from his reborn white-clothed head, wavers:
to temple, praise a God he's just befriended,
or the chubbying wife's bed he misses more?

Nothing to do and Varus to do it with. So
he shows me the girl he's doing (Petite salope,
I'd do her myself). As it does, when you talk to
anyone but a real whore, money comes up.
She wants to borrow my car, I refuse her,
not letting on I don't have one—only show
strength before the women. Always lie well.

FREUD IN TORONTO

Sometimes I must remember I'm
not a ten-year-old Korean girl
in a Sunday air-force-blue Baptist
dress. Or whoever else is talking
now. In the hardware store in
February, just between winds,
they're out of faucets. I buy
sandpaper, twine, and carpet
tacks anyway, and apologize.

THE SHOW
TO
END ALL

Socrates down the log flume, toga windblown white;
Jesus, losing at bumper cars, asks Himself
in Joual, *What would Judas do?. . . He was always
rather good at this.* Buddha and Ghandi each
outshooting the other at the BB-gun stand,
trying to win a stuffed panda doll and
the affection of a tired Lilith. Moses,
Mohammed argue in the lost pan-Semitic
slang, is it sherbet, sorbet, or sorbé? W. C. Fields
hawks tickets to Confucius and Lao Tzu—
two rubes if he ever saw them—for the tent
where scant-dressed girls prong overfed panthers
through low hoops. Descartes, lost deep in
the bleachers, doesn't know what to think.

We all hope to believe
what every cartoon and scripture says,
though this freak show is a brief world
we have the unique best thing to offer.
Maybe it's true, once some kid won, perhaps,
some playground horking contest,
or was fastest to say The Lord's Prayer
in Pig Latin.
What does it matter there are seven billion talents
without Nobels or a World Cup, cachet or posterity,
if I have mine?
Here's to the world's most incontinent dodgeball player,
how he can weave a throw
as a yellow snake through the gym floor.

WORLD'S LARGEST CABBAGE MOTH COLLECTION

for Vladimir Nabokov

Once engrossed he picked a flower,
was hound-and-foxed through the rest of childhood,
trapped by bigger boys more white than his mute skin:
netted by hands, pinned against brick schoolyard walls.
Still when they danced the flick knife on his neck
as if to prick and suck the life out
there was always something
desperate, fluttering in their eyes.
They too needed him,
and he held on to this,
even in February when they packed
fairy-tale white snow into his underpants.
Now his vengeance is clinical, Roman:
he pins to pleasant-smelling wood cases
the formalin-soaked specimens
of the world's largest cabbage moth collection.

WORLD'S LARGEST PIÑATA

Hale children gather amid further ado
near mantra places: Transcona, Red Deer,
Nepean. They are so tanned from riding horse
you can barely tell them from the Cree.
They're all here in the park with cows and parents
to see who'll break the world's largest piñata.
He'll get the cosseting trip to Cancún
and return affirming suburban myths,
such polite people! Sponsored
by the Pangloss Club, this trip
will open a door to better appreciation
of hot peppers, bribe and taxation systems,
everything but the smell of tripe frying
and why the dogs follow him everywhere.

I did not win. Instead of the beach
I went to some town of a seven-foot name and thought
poverty explained the broken glass atop walled fences.
There are no eager retrievers named Petula,
dogs lie in gutters, vultures keep off
if only for fear of the living and shame
to eat anything that should have been named.

Back in the True North there are smarter ravens
and poverty is clever enough to hide in ground beef,
well water, populist parties sponsored by cable companies,
cheerful postage stamps celebrating Wonder Bread.
This is also Cuchulain's kingdom, Canute's Canada:
we are all huddled south waving our staffs
at the world's largest piñata.

WORLD'S OLDEST TOAST

for Ben Zaretsky

Sure they'd said, back
in the accordion country,
that this was the place
of opportunity, gilded land.
What did our parents know?
The most wealthy here don't
even own a pewter samovar.
Ohn a chainik mir
zind gor nisht, oremer leit.

So on the day my daughter, your grandmother,
was born—the first thing we liked about
the New World—my wife Chana saved
a piece of toast. There wasn't
enough money for bronzed booties.

It's the only thing you have of hers.
It was revered unbuttered through
the Depression, Yalta, miniskirts,
nuclear families with fallout shelters,
and the many years of my burial.

It is a few days before Passover,
the day Chana was born, and your mother
wants to burn it, invent her own Exodus
and Genesis.

WORLD'S PENULTIMATE PASSENGER PIGEON

for Martha

They say I'm the end of my kind.
They don't know when almost asleep
I heard last night for the first time
in more migrations than I can count
a distant nephew's wings whistling.

This dawn, feral pigeons, poor grey trash,
dropped by again to mock me
with their strange European accents.
Later, gangs of the collector ape
who walks upright, like the magpie,
come too. They point and hoot at
the all-fours apes in their cages.
But before my roost they stand
quiet, some take off their plumes,
run their skinny flightless wings
through their bared thin crests,
heads bow, they look at their talons,
white ruffs are adjusted, the ape-chicks
hushed as their parents think about. . .
what? Their own endings?

With all this mateless time chained
to my perch, waiting to be ate,
I've learnt to use the hidden parts
of my little dove brain,
taught myself some of the humans' song
with the help of the old parrot next door
and the soothing tones of the one who feeds me.
His song is *Maaar-tha, Maaar-tha.*

One makes do. Still, on the whole I'd
rather not be in a Cincinnati zoo,
and so I sleep fictions,
forests between rivers,
pray to the goddess Paloma
to send me to the flocks
now massed only
in two small memories.

WORLD'S GREATEST THIEF

A clever man siphoned rounded-off interest
into the realer crags of a Swiss account:
few answers, no questioning,
till Interpol pinned him by its digits.
My crime leaves no pawprints:
wandering urgent, white palliative wards
with their smell of apricots and lost campaigns,
pinch tunes from the dyings' last thoughts,
a soul-music thief, ghoul of remainders.

WORLD'S OLDEST RAT

for Tallulah

After 32 years of back lanes changed past his ken,
until he doesn't know if he's moved or lived in the
same manhole all through time, you'd expect more
dignity: it befits his hard-won girth and the scrapes
with cat and fox. Yes, even he can see God's purpose
in the trail of not quite cleaned bones, but night's
best believer does not know why his teeth ice up
as he gnaws through canvas, furred knees locking
at every old leap so bad he forgets to squeal.

TENT OF SCIAMATIFIC WONDERS

In the tent of sciamatific wonders
the horn-rimmed inventor
of the self-lighting cigarette
waves perfunctorily at his brainstorms.
You've probably seen the infomercials:
the automated toe-clipper caddy;
kissing machine; rodent
proximity detector; the device
that blocks the device
that counteracts the
device that blocks your phone number;
and his favourite, the machine
that invents its own purposes.

DEATH'S TENT

Yes, we've all seen It
in felled warblers near Lansdowne,
slept past mid-week alarms.
But now for the Real Nothing.
Barnum's apprentice
ushers us with macabre spiel
into Death's tent,
The show to end all
through a dim, humid passage
and machine-made fog into
nothing but bare backs
of canvas tent-flaps twisting
confusedly to the parking lot.

BABY
BEEF

GREE-CEE SPOON

for John Stiles

We're all here alone because:
in the other place they're skint,
sell tomato by anaemic slice.

Here we have Emily Carr–
style paintings of Greek ruins
in Irish monochrome green.

Walls *peach in colour*,
the zaftig waitresses
tally ring fingers.

Two men too old not to argue
can't decide the difference
between veal and baby beef.

A heavy-eyes horsehaired chick
smoking, nods as to imaginary
friends inside the candy music.

Three men quickly agree:
the massage parlour next,
if you don't mind Chinese.

Sweeter than home fries with
ketchup, an arms-length couple
kisses in their sign language.

Both us anxious to pack, get away: and I,
new to being in The South, being this white,
think rummaging distracted I accidentally stole
her father's toothbrush. More Freudian
yet: he with falsetto rusted clippers
trimming the Christian yew bush.
So this is what she wanted to leave.
Me in her girlhood postered bed,
she in her younger sister's room.

Is that the interstate?
Ink-smudged outsider art
of pine after hemlock pass.
Still I pine after the driver,
none of this strange to her:
old red Chevies everywhere,
nopal cacti surprised by flash frost,
my childhood weather, flannel-
print sleeping arrangements.

In Brazil they repeat to say *yes*, I'm told.
The Carolina parakeet went extinct,
saw its colours once in still museum cases,
here they repeat to deny. On the radio
Sir Paul McCartney. The knight from
the *White Album* reminding us to do
it in public places. Easy for him to
do it in the road, no Sam-Browned
state troopers in Liverpool. We sing
along, but she doesn't agree much.

Virginia tarmac rambles
giant ahead as the Saturday paper,
Entertainment, Opinion,
Cars, Food, Lodging.
Signs warn: Though smoking's a liberty,
there is no room for irony and
don't drive on the paved shoulder,
chain gang ahead, only
white men hold shotguns.

Some day, she predicts,
fake prison uniforms will be fashionable.
Again? They must have been once,
in the duck-tailed age of Elvis.
More white-on-green headlines, detours.
Richmond, Bumpass, Onancock:
pathetic but no fallacy,
check the map if you like.

But there's a pancake house ahead,
Let's stop, a snake-handling church
on the Winston-Salem road,
and still no billboards explain
dogs lying in roadside state.
Truck or gun? Is their Cerberus
a three-headed human?

In a red plastic wicker basket—unsweet
corn doughnuts they call hush puppies.

THAI RESTAURANT

Before food, Spadina.
A light woman bemused,
small bags drip out
large plastic one,
shouts at me *English bones*.
My stomach has other dreams.

Later alone, Thai restaurant,
by the door. In a jar,
on a teak ceremonial barge,
mothballs flown in maybe from—
no wait, they're Scotch mints.
Tables so close together,
wrong-timed laughter blushes
edible garnish. A dark woman,
English, a few seats over,
her mane, shawl cascade.
Her man with black clotted hair
has foreign parents, therefore belongs.

Hasn't come yet, I am waiting still
for perfect release, the mouth-burst
of self-contained button mushrooms:
mine's the cilantro and green chicken.

Maybe it will not come at all.
The couple monsoons past me,
waying out at-the-same-time-not-together,
she carrying a poster, Forgotten Paris Ca. 1962,
ring of steel or carbon dates her fingers,
or like a tree her own face rings.
Two of the rings peeking at me,
a racoon.

Such times I miss my bones
alone, drinking like a stranger
in the St. Martin's cemetery café.

ETHIOPIAN RESTAURANT

The Ethiopian restaurant's
always waited past the park,
near my place, even before you.

Hungry and reaching for
close quick comfort, I
suggest it, my first trial. Why?

The party was good,
there was blue cheese
and a private joke
at the celebrity host's expense.
I smile, but not until
I see the flimsy menu,
try *injera* done three ways. Why?

No sense of humour, I know.
Maybe because I was too hungry
to see you were beside me.
Now it is all right, red lentils super,
we are sharing a thick mango drink.

Or because when I was eight,
a tall Jew from Ethiopia,
Baruch (means "blessing"),
stayed at our house, told us how
he fled a regime, like Moses,
across four days' desert into Sudan.
Baruch, the first black man I met,
at the age all male guests
are uncles, was a Brother.

Or, because peeking at the corner store
wondering *Is it open to buy roach traps
for your kitchen?* I see
on the restaurant window
the Ethiopian word for star
is the same as the Hebrew.

It is a short walk to another
convenience store with bug bait.

We go to your place. They die.

I try. But you cannot know
how glad I am to have eaten
among tall, lean, dark people.

VIETNAMESE RESTAURANT

I'm keeping records in case—
for the day we don't kiss.

Pace Dad, not everything
is pork here, I settle on
beef soup with noodles
and what looks like
a whole cow tongue.

One guy behind me is complaining,
his companion is more reasonable,
But not everything is Jewish. Maybe
not even the view I have
of the owner's tank, the goldfish,
or Goldfarb Goldblatt Goldman.
The only yellow here is the split pod
of the bean sprouts. No clue
if they're to put in the soup, or
meant to munch on before.
The only natives are done,
or they just got here, or want
only tea. The only natives are
the white cat and the bronze
Buddhist prosperity statue.
(These Viet Cong
are capitalist, religious.)

Behind me the Canadians say
. . . only 40% off. . . The American Girl,
and the Eye-Rainy-In guy
I axadenally thought
was Pakistani. . . The problem is
those jerkoffs at home,
six hours choosing their pants.

What was her name?
At that summer school
I sat next to Reezwan
learning French again,
the Vietnamese girl too
learning one of both
our official tongues, both
screamed at her parents
by the buzzcuts who fought there?
Through the white cotton blouse,
thick for July, the thoughtful nipples?
My memory turns up no name,
in its vagueness a paedophile.
It must be the soup. Caught
myself staring at the girl
talking to her aunt
behind the Wasserstein
watertank the Goldfisch
in the same brief explosions
as the limy hot soup.

Caught myself doing
too much thinking,
must be brought on
by the girl at the poetry reading,
looked like you. And each lime,
as you love in your Coke,
one of the solid floating things
to bring flimsy lands together.

I'll never finish this tongue.
Every day I forget more French,
it is too late to learn everything anew.
The stew's tongue is Jewish,
the hot peppers are Mexican,
at the reading the girl
was you, so I got her number.
And last night the man I almost punched
who thinks he brought us together
as if I hadn't noticed your thighs yet.

Years ago now, with an ex-ex
in Washington, we saw a tribute
to the Vietnam Incident, oddly
none to the two World Wars.
Perhaps there was too much to say
even in slabs of marble. Vietnam,
Washington: the country of
their defeat. Here I am near Fort York,
a place the Yanks once burnt to the ground.
I'm eating hot phó, not talking to my neighbours
about their racial theories, if only because
my tongue hurts.

OUTSIDE A MEXICAN CAFÉ

Poor Carmelita: underaged siren of the menu,
a monastic name. Or maybe it was Cenicienta.

But you're selling food with two-thirds breasts,
narrow jeans. What family insanities urge

you show your buns to sell burgers? You lead me
to eat, clutch my shirt tentatively—cotton salvation.

A clutch may be worse than liberty.

You've suffered the bleeding a few years,
your commercial femininity. Grandmother

makes tortillas, the two sisters at their brooms.
Of course your mother watches tables, you:

Tighter, Carmelita.

STREET VENDORS

Mistake dreaded later for weeks, even
the doctor could not say the Latin title
of this taco-lurking Aztec hex. Hypos
in my each southern hemisphere,
Monday left Tuesday right painful etcs.

But it fills fiesta hunger for: St.
Something, didn't catch. The town's
feast day. Even the furthest lamplight
is streamered in Catholic tricolour.
The least effective fireworks sent
Sputniking, a hoarse Saint
Catherine's wheel murmuring
aside the peeled wooden scaffold
between town square and church.
In this two-cactus joint, easier
to find a tequila than its patron.

Others roasting maybe just peanuts
and corn, they have no Guy Fawkes,
but fire everywhere newly orders
things, strikers' pillowed heads
tomorrow will forget to picket, won't recall
there's no work today to siesta skip.

STANDARD CURRY

English provincial Standard Curry
and a French film in grey Jericho,
on a brisk walk up the Woodstock Road,
you told me it was your first Indian.
I said you were better looking than her.
We spoke over tea and Econobiscuits,
of all we were since we met
over a computer we'll outlive twenty times
and the fog-thick ragged dictionary.
I don't think *fuck* was in it, but I explained
fuddle-duddle to you, trying
too hard to be clever, I wondered
was *trou d'eau* a hole in the water?
Built a weak bridge over oceans.
Nearly two in this Oxford Blue morning,
stars shone through Thames Valley cloud
in that conjuror Berkeley's slideshow.

I asked whether you were too Muslim to be kissed:
the only time I was glad you said *no*,
you in your half-shut doorway.
Two nights later we tried pints of bitter,
the joyful mess of your smoked floor,
where you finally traded your Camels
for my ass, if only for the night.

You fuddle-duddled off back to Asia. I,
always looking for higher definition,
fell upon vanillin waifs and greedy thinkers,
or waited that they fall on me.

LEIBNIZ COOKIES

No sleep: last night
the neighbour *zubzubbing*
his girlfriend, who's
usually a telephone, but
seemed too real down
in the heating duct.

Before we met I liked
Leibniz, agreed we all
are mirrors of the same
Franklin Mint gewgaw.

One possible me is still
making love to you in U.K.,
a land that both exists and not.
This possible you at the
art school learning how the
16th-century dead painted
before there was a 17th
and death was immaterial,
a misunderstanding.

ICED TEA

It's true.
The perfect arrangement of the coleslaw
made you cry after the brief funeral,
though you're really in here to piss
like a camel. But there's knocking
and iced tea.

MONOPOLY COFFEE SHOP

Ten years since I saw your brown hair
last, at the interview I thought I flubbed.
You were through the thick glass of
the Monopoly Coffee Shop, grey
March afternooning with your cousin.

Of course it was I who recognized,
long after last repeating your name
with my lower brain. Your jaw
fell a sycamore's mace: *Him, did I
once see a leer through his phone voice?*

We traded *you look goods* but you were
shorter, more righteous, leaving for
an arid seminary to study the obscure
ancient art of not loving. Your breasts,
once famous pears, had shrunk a decade.

The anonymous note, yes, that was mine,
N. helped me write the willow-tree poem.
In Israel there will be few orchards.
I did not ask for your overseas number,
happy to see your tongue if only once.

MONKS'
FRUIT

JERICHO

Oxford, 1999

By boding church of Jericho,
down and every out of the way,
past flecking brick canalside works
the people dredge what they don't say,
and mince their meat to spend their perks:
but spoke their wheels each rare clean day,
down and every out of the way.

Just off from Brize to Kosovo,
up and painful in God's side,
like hunting namesake birds explode
two Harrier bombers. British pride
will teach Slavs English with payload—
as if to save Albanian hide!
Somewhat up in God's right side.

Artifizial, sniffs the tourist, unimpressed
by *The Golden Hinde* or *The Panting Harte*
or whatever recreated galleon I'm on,
my last week in England.

And a babe she is:
the maidenhead
is virtuous as a shanty,
although root beer in hue,
she creaks only in pleasure.
Who can deny her?
The tidal Thames licks her
while the white kittiwake
and black, dagger-necked shag
look her over.

A holiday note on recreations:
a philosopher, I don't care which,
from his paper tower said: a god
recreates the world anew every moment.

Good enough for me.
Maybe in the British Museum
or in Berlin they have
the original Athenian cedar ship,
with no such orange trim.

The Golden Hinde seated
tenuous on the edge of
the other, rounded bank
of the Big Smoke: hold
her gunwales, caress, feel
her pirate past and in tar
the making of a knighthood
and an England, very anti-Europe.

The German takes photos anyway.

The bottom of the London I know.
The *Hinde* to grab the world from.

MULROONEY

Two lads' fifth drunkenness,
bright-framed eyes on benches
across from the Hungarian Centre.
Indoors, people learning ethnic glee:
Saturday, it is a rugby shirt never
meant to seem washed.

> *Hell with mind over manna,*
> *this is cognitivodka.*

Mulrooney slurs me his middle name
which is, of all things, Aloysius. The
Christian Brothers called him that,
his crawly saint-name, till he graduated
to drawing welfare in Southwark.

FLORIANÓPOLIS

I'm not looking at the Brazilian girl
on the bench near the cigarette stand.
I'm just watching her glance under the
great boughs of the venerable white fig,
under the same sky as the circling vultures,
high black dreidels praying *Something please die.*
In the cathedral's shadow we too pray, each in
our own language and faith, for someone to live.

SOR JUANA

A nun's apprentice sits among the fields at sunset,
plucking the clovers of God.
Bemired creeks run through, strewn casually with
castors, acacia, crumbled brick.

Sisters are taught to care. She nurses her rosary.
A meagre dog looks on her frock:
Her clothing is hot, and she is stingy and plain.
He chases a lizard for her supper.

MAGIC MEXICO

The dark pretty witch hung tastesome artistically
nude photos of herself over the bedroom door. Inside
was a bed smelling of pomegranate. They said
It's a spiritual place.

Still, nothing in Magic Mexico is like visions,
lizards hide under wild watermelon vines,
cactus pears fall without remorse,
nightly bar-Oooming from the artillery range
of the out-of-shape *Ejercito Mexicano*
gets in the way of tantric sex. Not even
the black hawk or vulture will discuss
their near sky, ancient spirits with me.

DATES

I

A sprayed night on Prince Arthur,
God at his *toilette* with perfume atomizer or
maybe gardening. On the street liking you
even more than the thought of first date,
seeing your bared calves,
the perfect curvature
of night and women.
Your choice of drink
a geography, a
somewhere giggle:
I have to joke
about the vintage tin ad.
Anything else is too early,
quick taxi ride, a peck:
first McIntosh bite waiting.

II

In the wrong restaurant you swayed into me
through your strand of mouth-searching hair,
sexable floating gravity, time-saving pendulum.
Later that Thursday night party
holy with wine, your boss
smiles, cake with salad and I,
too polite, talked to the grey cat
and the drunk radio dyke linguist.
Your prairie-flat vowels
addictive comfort,
your nails apricots.

This time the walk home is wind,
downhill south wearing a topsail of a green jacket,
defence against blown sand. Teeming home too:
a black leather superstition of youth
on Dupont from a bar, their palladium.
Their time, 2:00 A.M. My time's the
just-earlier smudge, you
a step above me, mouths equal,
nudged so unlike Toronto.
Your laugh to last me days from
the right kiss, you didn't mind,
I in a new smile. I am learning
lasting wax patiences from you,
one's a cheerful gesture with
two hands I can't pronounce.

WAINSCOTING

Look, about the wainscoting:
I like it here but am thinking,
next time, a dive with cheap fat wings
on white plastic plates with blue circles.
You will look even better next to them.
Big do here, tavern downtown, brown
original brick exterior. Silent, fleshy,
next-booth couple owls us over trying
to remember how they began, what to order.
Their eyes commute in two-on-twos,
from hockey game to wainscoting.

OVERTIME

Because we are young and know
the meaning of *rondelle* but not
value-added, overtime is blessed

one whistle and we go from the end
of the game to a new one, where
anything can happen for 5 minutes.

GOING WEST

The West train. We've
rode this before, your
sister's place, the town
where everyone's glad
they're born so white.

Last night we're in
High Park, July green
lusher than your past
Vancouver days. Frog,
bats, chipmunk, heron,

and sleeping mallards.
Tonight not sleeping
with you, though I
would rather. Instead,
to the west burbs

to comfort P. on
his father's cancer.
Of course I'm tired,
largely too young
to think about

strangers' mortality,
rather be back at
your place. This
morning at mine,
after love, washing I

noticed blood, didn't
tell you, I think it's
too early in the month
for that, I'd still rather
the blood be yours.

Summer: new life is
the furthest thing
from my mind.
Tests? In England,
at the clinic, the

Islamic nurse approved
of circumcision.
For once a road map
to Mid East peace:
blood and trains.

But *I'm going west*,
they said in WWI,
when they meant
in pieces, home
in a body bag.

Going west I
just passed the
park, then the
perfect lips of
the Humber,

soccer fields, dogs
walking men, boys
on green bicycles
swarming nude hills
like clothed ants.

Seven-twenty-something in the evening.
This is the hour for planning regret.
Close couples scrape silver over china,
the suburbans joke about accident,
clack of their kissing teeth. Softer now.
Even in winter there's something not-grey,
a dog, child, patio extension in their garden,
or feeders with crossbills.

This is also the hour of acceptance. Grace
in Saskatchewan blesses Cargill, Monsanto:
I blur between espresso Zen and
cowardice, not saying anything
to the snide face behind
the station wicket, watching
as the window reverses positions,
he with the cash, I
the right to travel unhindered.

LENT

A Glasgow-coloured leadenness
has come between. I am not the
slow ox who chattered about your
skin without saying anything.

Not he who, remembering the vowelless
names of your family, which cousin
dangled the golden condom earrings,
could be easy as you or as harelike.

The plumbous is in my bile, worse
than pain. The Lenten spirit has
entered the heart's chambers that
turned, like stale coffee, liverish.

CRABAPPLES

All yesterday morning the birds
were dancing around the Dominican
orchard, singing through crabapples,
just on the far side of my place.
You live on the close side, north-
west, but never too close. Dance
with me in the fallen monks' fruit;
alive like sparrows, and the blue-
yellow birds the perverse Anglais
call *tits*. We'll mock the Blackfriars,
steal bougies at Notre Dame, and
pelt the Virgin of Guadalupe
right in the watermelon: hail
Mary with them, true right
to the touchdown line.

But they hail Mary when
there's no hope left.

I want to share a pulpy past,
a seven-year-old's crabapples.
And the tangy, fibrous
future with you.

BOTANY

It doesn't help to know the willow
in its passive-aggressive quiet
is glad behind its grave droops:
no amount of drowning or hanging
can kill it off. Even crude hearts,
if carved into its bole with care,
will not harm it. What use is botany
with no money or you? This tree
doesn't give a damn I was your
flower-monkey. Must be why Iroquois
ate its quiet bark to cool their pangs.

FERNS

for Diputado Marco Rascón

In Mexico the elected ones
put sand in their coffins
stormed the assembly
wearing pig costumes.
They choose not to die.

That was why we stopped
loving each other. And
the *anís* and your boredom
looked still more Spanish
as the night was dying.
Searching for ferns
in each others' hair
we found only
things to set afire.

EXODUS 19

You promised the use
of creamy eagles
to find home.

Your weak soaring thing
planes, hounded by gulls
spooked by osprey

taunted by crows, and swoops
to fish quail from dried wadis
away from the shadow of man.

ANCESTORS

X

You, dead mothers, never imagined me here and not in
your North England making shingles to buy ale, bread,
leek, and mutton. Your tribe: wandering Christians sent
by Cromwell to the Thirteen Colonies. (Good turncoats!
You later fled them for King George.) This when Oliver
let the Jews back into England after 400 years, missing
Chaucer, Agincourt, Reformation, sacred Shakespeare.

Y

Brave-headed sons of time, you pretended to be
farmers, went west, raised good onions and hens
surrounded by their barley and oats. In a place flat,
far-sighted as Manitoba, it *is* hard not to steal ideas.
White took from Cree; and you, from White Russia,
lifted off that German Marx's theories of workers,
never suspecting so clumsy a novelist might be lying.

ACKNOWLEDGEMENTS

The author wishes to thank the following for their help with *Monks' Fruit*:

Jonathan Bennett, Avril Bruten, Sedef Çokay, Lenore Langs, Dennis Lee, Gav Levin, rob mclennan, George Murray, Ariadne Patsiopoulos, K. I. Press, Jana Prikryl, Julie Roorda, Rebecca Seiferle, Martha Sharpe, John Stiles, Sean Tai, Paul Vermeersch, Sarah Wall, Sarah Whatmough, Carleton Wilson, Silas White, His Holiness Pope John Paul II, Patrick Woodcock and Yehudit.

The author is also grateful to the following magazines:

"Catullus — Poem 10" was the winner of the Nelson Reese Poetry Prize (2002) and was published as a broadside in the "poem" series (#156) by above/ground press. Thanks to Nathaniel G. Moore and rob mclennan.

"Death's Tent" appeared in *Literary Review of Canada*, Summer 2001.

"Magic Mexico" appeared in *Pagitica* magazine, Vol. 2 No. 1, Winter 2002.

"Moses" appeared in *echolocation*, Vol. 1, No. 1, 2003. Thanks to Triny Finlay/*echolocation*.

"Outside a Mexican Café" appeared in slightly different form in *Wayzgoose Anthology 8* (1997).

"Standard Curry" appeared in *Literary Review of Canada*, February 2002.

"World's Best Thief" was published in *The Hamilton Examiner/Exit* magazine (now *Women's Times*), June 2001.

"World's Largest Cabbage Moth Collection," "World's Largest Piñata," and "World's Oldest Rat" appeared in *The Drunken Boat*, summer 2001 <www.thedrunkenboat.com>.

"World's Oldest Toast" first appeared in *Literary Review of Canada*, June 2003.

Some of the poems herein were published, often in slightly different form, in my two chapbooks *Freak Show* (above/ground press, Ottawa, 2001) and *Restaurant Reviews* (Junction Books, Toronto, 2001).

The phrase "peach in colour" is taken from the poem "How yah doon anight?" by John Stiles, and is used with his kind permission. Copyright © John Stiles 2003.

The author wishes to thank the Toronto Arts Council for its support of this book in the form of a Level 1 Grant. The author also wishes to thank the Ontario Arts Council for a Works in Progress Grant.

Karen Press

ABOUT THE AUTHOR

A. J. Levin was born in Winnipeg during a Halloween blizzard. He has also lived in Montreal, Mexico and England. He took a B.A. at the University of Toronto and an M.Phil. at St. Hugh's College, Oxford, and served as the Junior Dean at St. Cross College. He is the author of two chapbooks, and now lives in Toronto.

A Junction Book

Typeset in TEFF Collis

TEFF Collis was designed in 1993 by Christoph Noordzij for The Enschedé Font Foundry.

Printed and bound in Canada

EDITOR
Jana Prikryl

EDITOR FOR THE PRESS
Carleton Wilson

TYPESETTING
Carleton Wilson

COVER DESIGN
Carleton Wilson

COVER ART
Detail of *Virgin of Guadalupe*

Junction Books
568 Indian Grove · Toronto, ON · M6P 2J4
www.junctionbooks.com

Nightwood Editions
www.nightwoodeditions.com